MARKETING YOURSELF TO THE REAL WORLD

10 SIMPLE STEPS
to gain a competitive edge
in the job market

SUSAN CAPLAN

MARKETING YOURSELF TO THE REAL WORLD

Copyright © 2009 by Susan Caplan

Book design by Andrew Twigg Design Studio.

Printed in the United States of America.

Library of Congress Control Number: 2009908347

ISBN-10: 0-9824780-0-3

ISBN-13: 978-0-982-4780-0-4

This book is dedicated to my parents, who gave me a solid foundation, courage and passion. Thank you for giving me "roots and wings."

CONTENTS

Introduction

I speak at various businesses, associations and universities about marketing communications. I started to notice a pattern in the questions I was getting from students at the universities. The questions weren't about marketing but about the job search process: what to say, what to do, how to act, how to gain an edge over the competition. I told them about "marketing themselves" during their job search. They were surprised, excited and energized by the results…because this strategy works!

So I've put these thoughts together in this book. I've taken the skills I have seen work in business marketing and linked them with tools, ideas, tips and powerful guidelines to help you market yourself to the real world. They will all build on each other to give you an edge in the job search process.

This book is a compilation of marketing ideas, thoughts, observations and strategies that are based on my professional expertise. A special "thank you" to the many professionals who provided their input throughout.

This is a new start, a new world, a new experience.

Chapter 1

The Warm-Up
(Marketing Yourself)

When you move from school to "the real world," it is a huge transition. For the first time in your life, your success won't be determined by grades, and time won't be measured by semesters. Getting the career you want takes some preparation. Once the preparation is complete, you can move forward.

Marketing YOU

Marketing is about buying or selling a product or service in the marketplace. That is what you're doing in your job search, except YOU are the product. And you are taking yourself to market to sell.

Your slate is clean. YOU decide what you want your future to hold. YOU decide what the road should look like. YOU decide the outcome. Get it? It's about YOU, YOU, YOU.

You want to be the one people remember when there's an

opportunity. You want to be the one people remember when they need the best person for a job. You don't want to blend in with everyone else; you want to make yourself stand out.

Repackage Yourself

Start thinking of yourself as a product—a product that is going to market and needs to be sold to make money. Repackage yourself as if you were selling a product. If you think about it, it has taken the last 20 years to produce this product of YOU as you are today. Now you're ready to go to market and need to reinvent your image to take the next step. You're slightly reworking the product to fit in the job market.

You are no longer a college student, but you're not quite part of the working population either. This is a great place in your life to start thinking of yourself as two separate people. *One is the personal side,* and may not change much from what you are now. *The other is your professional side,* the one that is looking to start a career. And, yes, there is certain packaging that needs to take place to sell YOU in the professional world. In some cases there may only need to be slight changes to your personal side to make way for your professional side. Over time you'll be able to blend the two.

You will take chances and try new things…some may work and some may not. Over time, you'll figure out what makes up "YOU" as the product among the thousands of other people (products) in the marketplace. That's why marketing yourself is so critical.

It's OK to draw oUtSiDe the lines

There are people that you see in the media that have learned to draw outside the lines to get noticed. Think about the most popular rock stars, TV stars or movie stars who come to mind immediately. With hundreds of singers and actors out there, the ones who you think about quickly just found ways to stand out and be a little different from everyone else. They have packaged themselves and their products to be unique in the marketplace.

You are the key spokesperson for your product, YOU. But you don't have to be famous to have personal branding. It's the little things that allow some individuals to stand out from others. Find ways to differentiate yourself from everyone else. The most creative people usually stand out from the rest and get the attention. So while you are like so many others looking for a job, decide what makes you different. Thinking and acting strategically in this process will keep you ahead of the competition.

"The whole job search is so frightening; I don't know where to start. I don't even know how to talk to people. So how do I know if I'm doing it right?"

Student

TO DO

☐ Start thinking of yourself as a product

☐ Find ways to differentiate yourself from everyone else

Chapter 2

Becoming Purple

Remember, marketing yourself is about being noticed in the marketplace that you want to work. You want to be different from the others. You want to make an impression. You want to become purple, (or whatever your favorite color is that stands out) instead of gray (or whatever your least favorite color is that wouldn't stand out). What does this mean? It's that place that says, "I'm different." If you look at all the people looking for jobs, or the hundreds of people you've met, they all start to look the same. I call it "looking gray." Very few stand out. Remember in the last chapter we talked about celebrities who stand out? They became purple in their specific industry.

Make an Impression

Marketing yourself is about image, perception and reputation. I will be repeating this concept throughout the book because it's critical that you understand this. You need to package yourself to make the impression you want.

What does it take to make an impression? People get an impression of you from what they see, hear and decide about you in an instant…their image and perception of you. I've heard some people say that interviewers make a decision about a candidate in the first five minutes, and some say it's less than that. Either way, it doesn't give you much time when selling YOU.

Develop a reputation

Yes, you do want to develop a reputation. A solid one. Right now you are one of thousands of graduates looking for jobs. And, granted, while you may have many earrings or a pink streak in your hair that makes you stand out, is that really the image you want to portray to get the job?

What you'll learn in the following steps is how to define your strengths, values, goals and personality in order to present yourself in a compelling, persuasive manner. Marketing YOU means learning to express yourself in a consistent manner that will allow you to create an effective image.

Life is full of challenges and can throw you some curve balls. Therefore, you have to have a plan if you want to have any hope of staying on track. This book will teach you how to present yourself in the best possible way.

Be yourself, be strong, be confident.

TO DO

☐ Think of ways in which you can make an impression

Chapter 3

The Starting Line

You will be working on your marketing plan throughout the book. Setting up your job search is like putting together a map. Think about it this way; if you wanted to drive from California to New York, you'd plot out your route ahead of time. Otherwise you could take the wrong road or get lost. It's the same with your job search effort. You want to make sure you have a finish line or a destination and a plan for getting there. Each chapter of this book will add one more piece to help get you to your destination.

Marketing isn't something that's done once and then finished. Marketing YOU has to become your passion…it has to become an attitude. Think about the product you're selling, list the industry that fits your product and decide where you want to sell your product YOU.

Leave nothing to chance. Make your job search strategic. It takes some work, but you can't move forward without this effort. Let's get started, step by step, in creating your plan.

Step 1: Your Image

Take some time to think about how you may be seen by someone looking to fill a position. It's hard to see ourselves objectively. But if you're going to go into the professional world, you need to decide what your image will be and how you're going to get others to see you that way.

Start by writing down what you think your professional image is now. What do you look like? How are you perceived? Do you speak in complete sentences? Do you start each sentence with the word "like"? Do you look people in the eye when they talk to you? Do you play with your hair?

Next, write down what you would like your image to be. Do you want to look like a professional in a suit? Is your desired industry more creative? Does your college look work in the professional world? Think about what your competition looks like.

EXAMPLE

YOUR IMAGE

List the words that describe your current image. Then think about where you see your career heading and list the words that describe the image of the professionals in that field.

What is my image now?	What is the image of the field I'm going into?
Creative	Sophisticated
Unique	Refined
Free spirited	Polished
Outgoing	
Responsible	

TIP:

It's always helpful to see how others view you and how they would describe you. Pick three people you trust and respect. Ask them to describe you in three words…or a sentence. Their answer could be that you are happy, fun and silly. Or it could be that you are smart, a leader and focused. This will give you an idea of the image you now portray and provide a good starting place for moving forward. Then list the way you want to be seen in the professional world.

Is the image you need to succeed in your field in sync with the image you have right now? Don't worry if they don't look the same; for most people they don't in the beginning. Everything doesn't have to be answered now as you will be tailoring your image as you move through the book. The most important thing is to know where you want to be.

Step 2: Your Skills

It's important to be acutely aware of your skills and your strengths — especially ones that give you an edge over the competition. It's easy to "think" you're better than the next guy, but it's more important to be able to articulate why you're better and back that up with facts.

Make a list of your greatest skills and strengths. You know, the things people have told you you're good at. Think about computer, project management, graphic design and other skills. What are your strengths? What are the things that make you feel good, special and strong?

TIP:

Think of the times you've excelled, been creative or come up with something unique. Think about all of the things you've "worked on" or "worked for" such as summer jobs, clubs or volunteering. What in your background can you bring to the table?

EXAMPLE

YOUR COMPETITIVE EDGE

What skills do I have?

Computer
Writing
Speaking
Graphic design
Teaching

What are my greatest strengths?

I get along well with people
I motivate people
I'm a good athlete
I'm organized
I work quickly and efficiently
I am trustworthy

What have I worked on in the past that shows my skills and strengths?

Served as President of fraternity or sorority

Worked on a charity event

Planned group events

Held a part-time job while in school that involved event planning

Review your list. Does it answer the question "How are you better then the competition?" or "What can you bring to the table that they can't?" In other words, "Why would/should someone choose me?"

TIP:

I have heard from recruiters that they are looking extensively for specific skills, such as critical thinking, interpersonal and conflict management skills, time management, listening, verbal and written communication. So if you find after writing your list that maybe you fall short in an area that your industry would value, go out and take a class. You can take writing, public speaking, computer and other classes at local colleges.

Step 3: Your Audience

The next thing to address on your plan is where you ultimately want to end up in your job search effort? What does the finish line look like? This is the audience that your entire plan will revolve around. Along the way you'll want to be flexible and open to new opportunities, but when starting out you'll want to be as specific as possible. For now, you will want to get your name out to this audience and let them you know that you're looking for a job. But first you need to identify the area that fits your product YOU.

Once you set this goal, ask yourself, what kind of people work in this area, how do they dress, what organizations do they belong to. Most importantly, what organizations do the people higher up belong to? All of this will help direct your networking efforts.

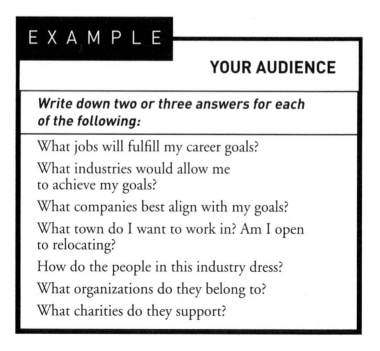

EXAMPLE

YOUR AUDIENCE

Write down two or three answers for each of the following:

What jobs will fulfill my career goals?

What industries would allow me to achieve my goals?

What companies best align with my goals?

What town do I want to work in? Am I open to relocating?

How do the people in this industry dress?

What organizations do they belong to?

What charities do they support?

Step 4: Measurement

A solid measurement system is an ongoing part of your plan. Every three months, review where you are and what you've achieved. Review what networking events you've attended and whether you've met the right people. Review the companies you've sent your resume to and if they've called you for an interview. If the results don't align with the finish line, change course. This will allow you to keep on track. You need to continually measure your results to achieve results.

TO DO

☐ Determine the image you want to portray

☐ Make a list of your skills

☐ Identify your target audience

☐ Set up a measurement system

Chapter 4

The Right Equipment
(Your Toolkit)

In the previous chapter, you identified your image, skills and audience. Remember, every step builds on the one before.

Now, using these steps, you can move forward and gather the tools you will need to build your toolkit. A construction worker can't go to a job site without his toolkit. He needs his hammer, screwdriver, etc. A football player can't go on the field to play without the proper equipment and gear. YOU cannot go to your job search without your toolkit.

The next step is the "branding" part of the job search. The following information will help you define yourself in your new professional role. Remember, you're selling a product… YOU. And with any product, you may need to develop packaging and tools to sell it. Keep that in mind as you work through the list. Also remember, the branding should reflect the professional you, not the personal you. Hopefully, over time, they will blend together.

Step 5: The Toolkit

Below are the tools you'll need for your job search. Everything listed below will help you portray a consistent, professional, sophisticated impression to your targeted audience.

TOOL: Business Card

I can't emphasize enough the importance of business cards in your job search effort. In fact, this may be the most important tool of your toolkit. Your business card is your first introduction of you as a professional. Get business cards made up immediately, have them with you at all times and hand them out to EVERYONE you meet. You never know who may be looking to hire or who will know someone else who is looking to hire.

Here are some specifics for your business card purchase:

- Purchase the best business card paper stock you can afford. You can go to a local print shop, or you can get them online, but do not buy cards with advertising on the back...it looks very unprofessional.

- Clearly display your name, phone number and email address.

- If you can afford it, do something to stand out from the thousands of other cards. That doesn't necessarily mean displaying a flower on them, unless you're looking to become a botanist. However, there are ways to keep your cards professional and make a statement. While one side will have your name, phone number and email address, the flipside can be a solid color...or put a small stripe along the bottom. This may be one way to allow people to identify you quickly.

- Somewhere on your card, put a tagline or list your skills (i.e. website designer, graphic artist, technology expert, marketing, creative, copywriter).

• Keep your cards in a business card holder. You don't want your cards to get frayed in your purse or pocket. You may not think that it matters, but if you hand someone a card with coffee stains on it or one that is torn or bent, it tells them that you're not organized or serious. This is not the impression you want to make.

TOOL: Phone Number

I mentioned above that you need to put your phone number on your card. You will also include this on your resume. Use a home phone number only if you are the only one checking messages. You can't expect your family or roommates to make the right impression. Otherwise, have a cell phone number, a dedicated voicemail number or a voicemail service that only you answer.

Check your voicemail or answering machine frequently and get back to anyone who leaves a message within in a few hours — 24 hours maximum. And make sure that your voicemail sounds professional. No music, no slang, no chewing gum while you're recording!

TOOL: Voice

Strive to make a good impression on the phone from the moment you answer it, or from the message you leave. Try to have all job-related conversations on a land line, not a cell, in order to minimize static and dropped calls. I've heard some people say that they will only talk on the phone if they are standing up, as it makes your voice sound stronger. You can try it. Remember to keep your full attention on your phone conversation. That means don't check email, text message or rummage through papers while on a call.

TIP:

We rarely hear our own voices, so take time to record your voice and listen to it over and over. Make sure you sound confident, direct, strong and in control so everyone you talk to will hear that as well.

TOOL: Email Address

Create an email address that sounds professional. Don't use your college nickname. A potential employer won't think much of you if they are sending a response to PartyGirl@xyz.com. If you can, set up a special email address with your name. For example, if your name is Mary Smith, then make your email address Mary@MarySmith.com. If you can't set that up, try putting your full name on one of the many other opportunities such as MarySmith@aol.com or MarySmith@yahoo.com. This way you can keep job-related messages from getting lost among your other emails. AND having an email address with your name on it makes it memorable and allows you to brand yourself in a professional way.

TOOL: Website

It is not critical for everyone to have a personal website. However, for those individuals whose work includes visual elements, this may be a good way to display work samples. Some examples of how a website may be useful are:

- If you're looking to be a graphic artist, display work you've done in the past or at school on your site.

- If you're someone who has had a great deal of press coverage of your work and you want to display the written reviews.

- If you've given speeches at events and want to show the pictures or video of your presentation.

Again, this may not be necessary for everyone, but when you're sending a follow-up email or an introductory email to someone, you can reference it.

TOOL: Resume and Cover Letter

Your resume and cover letter are very important. There are hundreds of books that can assist you with advice on how and what to write. In terms of marketing yourself and standing out, I will share a few thoughts:

- Like your business card, keep your resume in a folder. If it looks torn, stained or ragged around the edges, it will send the wrong message.

- Keep the overall look of your resume clean. And if you've come up with some type of branding (i.e. brown backing on your cards) you may include it here by placing a brown line across the top or bottom. But don't do too much to distract from your brand/ image.

- Proofread and check for spelling and grammar errors. NEVER have spelling errors in your resume. You will never get a second chance to fix this.

- When possible, try to tailor both your resume and your cover letter to the job you're applying for or to the type of position you want at a specific company or in a particular industry.

TIP:

Look up the website of the company you are applying to and carefully review the information. Try to relate your experiences in the cover letter to the information presented on their website. For example, you could mention an internship experience and how it ties into the company's mission or vision. Go back to Step 2 and review the list you already put together.

TOOL: Thank You Notes

Purchase a stack of thank you notes—not pink ones with balloons that you used at your 16th birthday party but professional notes to send out following a business meeting with someone. Why? Remember, we talked about making an impression, and you want to stand out. Many people do not take the time to do this. If you do, it's one more way to get your name in front of a potential employer.

While a handwritten note says a lot about you, it's okay to send an email instead. For companies you are especially interested in, you can send a quick thank you on your computer and then a handwritten note afterward. This way they will see your name twice after meeting with you and hopefully not forget you.

TIP:

If you do send a written note, make sure your handwriting is legible. Otherwise, you'll end up sending the wrong message.

And don't forget to send a thank you note to people who help you get a job or an interview. You may even want to send a gift or donation to a charity to show your appreciation. Remember, a big part about the job search is building relationships.

TOOL: Elevator Pitch

You're going to meet a lot of people during your job search. It's critical to be able to explain what you're looking for in a few succinct sentences. You should prepare a clear, easily understood statement about who you are, what you're looking for and what your competitive edge is. This has been referred to as an elevator pitch, meaning that you can deliver this in the time it takes to ride an elevator.

Now is a good time to go back to the list of skills you wrote in Step 2. Think of ways to insert them into your elevator pitch.

TIP:

Some people say your elevator pitch should take around 30 seconds, some say no more than two minutes. Usually it runs around 125 words. Practice this over and over. Ask people you respect to listen to your elevator pitch and give feedback.

TOOL: Job Search Log

Staying organized throughout the job search process is critical. You'll want to keep a log of everyone you've talked to, with their phone numbers and email addresses in one place. If you don't want to use an existing electronic program, create your own table with multiple columns for this information. Make sure to have a column for notes. Review it every week and highlight the people you want to follow up with. Note all conversations and dates and use this as a working tool. Being on top of your job search gives you an edge over everyone else.

EXAMPLE

JOB SEARCH LOG

Name	Company	Phone/ Email	Date Met/ Where	Notes
Joe Smith	B Corp	123-4567 Joe@bcorp. com	3/5 Chamber of Commerce Networking Event	Vice President of Marketing may be hiring in a few months.

TOOL: Time Management Schedule

Manage the job search process—don't let it manage you. This is part of the measurement process covered in Step 4. Set up a time management schedule for each week, listing all the tasks you'll need to do to make your job search successful. Make sure to set aside time for exercise and social events.

EXAMPLE

TIME MANAGEMENT SCHEDULE

Your schedule may include the following:

Daily:	1–2 calls to new companies or job opportunities
Daily:	2–3 calls/emails to follow up with individuals you've met
Daily:	Thank you notes to people you've interviewed with or who have recommended job opportunities to you
Daily:	2–3 resumes to new job opportunities
Daily:	Work out, eat well, talk with friends
Weekly:	1–2 networking events to attend
Weekly:	Meetings with people you've met to build relationships
Weekly:	1–2 interviews
Weekly:	Review of contact/measurement chart

> **TIP:**
> Try to schedule calls first thing in the morning so people can call you back all day. Also, try to make as many calls on Monday so you can schedule meetings for later in the week.

LAST BUT NOT LEAST...

TOOL: Your Online Image

Many companies are searching the Internet to find out about the individual they are considering for a job. Some of the places they may go are the various social networking sites. They want to find information about the individual, see what kind of image this person conveys and determine if the person is right for their company. Social networking sites are a great avenue to showcase your professional strengths so make sure to utilize them to your benefit.

You may have mentioned on your resume that you are interested in a specific area of business. The Internet offers many industry-related blogs that you can participate in and that place you in a good professional arena.

Or if you mentioned in your resume that you're active in a particular charity you may want to post videos of meetings, conversations with sponsors or even fundraising events you've worked on. This format portrays you as a team player and perhaps as a leader. Remember, the idea is to stand out from the thousands of other people looking for a job who have done nothing but write a resume.

TIP:

Remember, the web can be a place where image is established and spread quickly. It's up to you to determine what kind of image you want to convey online. Therefore, if the image of you is not conducive to your job search, then fix it. In other words, if there are pictures of you drinking with friends or pictures not showing YOU at your best, REMOVE THEM IMMEDIATELY. In addition, you may also want to be choosy about what people can read in your online profile. Remember to stay focused on the finish line.

"Once I had my toolkit in place, my job search was so much easier. It gave me the luxury of being able to focus on the job search and not having to recreate the wheel every time I went out to network or interview. I felt like I was in control."

Student

TO DO

Gather or create the following tools:

- ☐ Business Cards
- ☐ Voice Mail
- ☐ Phone Message
- ☐ Email Address
- ☐ Resume
- ☐ Cover Letter
- ☐ Thank You Notes
- ☐ Elevator Pitch
- ☐ Job Search Log
- ☐ Time Management Chart
- ☐ Online Image

Chapter 5

Packaging is Everything

Marketing yourself is about image, perception and reputation. Remember when I said that earlier? First impressions are very important. How you look when someone first meets you should create the right impression.

You will need a professional interview wardrobe. Take time to put together at least three "work" outfits that say you want the job. Make sure they are always clean, pressed and presentable. If you are not good at putting things together, go to a major department store with personal shoppers who will be happy to put together some outfits especially for you. The outfits don't have to be the most expensive, but spend as much as you can. This is (again) about marketing YOU and making a great first impression.

Step 6: Appearance

Below are suggestions about your appearance. Not everything I suggest applies to all industries, so use your judgment. Think of your target audience and dress accordingly.

Clothing:

- Both men and women should always wear a suit on their first interviews. I know that this is controversial and a lot of companies are casual, but unless the company specifically states not to, that's it…end of discussion. Once you start a job, you can make wardrobe adjustments.

- If you are going into an artistic or creative profession, you have more leeway, because how you are dressed will reflect on your skills.

- You should never look sloppy. Make sure your clothes are clean. Forget about, *"But this is who I am."* You're either interested in getting a job and making a good impression or not.

– NO jeans or anything denim

– NO T-shirts

– NO capri pants or shorts

– NO torn or wrinkled clothing

TIP:

Remember, it's about making an impression. It's always better to be overdressed to make that first impression. ALWAYS wear clothes that make you feel good about yourself.

Women:

- Always wear a suit. No mini-skirts. I would suggest keeping colors and patterns simple…they just seem to work better.

- The pantyhose issue is big right now and different companies have different policies. To be safe, wear them for your interviews. And bring an extra pair in case you tear them on your way there.

- Always wear a bra; don't show cleavage.

- Don't wear too much make-up. Remember, you want them to remember your talents and skills and the professional package you've put together, not your bright red lipstick.

- NO bare midriffs or short shirts that may periodically show your waste…even if it's under a jacket. It says you're not serious.

"I visit different colleges to interview graduating seniors. One time I was talking with a female candidate that had a short shirt on. Every time she moved her hands, her belly button ring would pop out. It was distracting and I didn't get to concentrate on what she was saying. She didn't get another interview."

Accounting Firm Recruiter

Men:

- Always wear a suit.

- When it comes to shirts and ties, keep the colors and patterns simple. Don't wear a tie with footballs or beer mugs on it, or a hot pink shirt. Keep everything conservative.

Hair:

- Make sure your hair is combed and in place. Don't wear your hair spiked or have purple stripes in it.

- Men, make sure you have a clean shave and if you have a beard, make sure it is trimmed.

- Women, don't have big hair for the interview. Make sure it's styled professionally.

Shoes:

- No canvas shoes should be worn on a job interview.

- No flip-flops.

- Have 2 to 3 pairs of shoes that you rotate so none look too worn out.

- Women, get comfortable shoes with low heels. Get at least two pair of black ones, as they go with everything. While sandals can be okay, it's better to wear closed-toe shoes for a sense of professionalism.

Jewelry:

- Don't wear any loud, flashy or glittery jewelry. If the jewelry is the first thing they see, or hear, then you're sending the wrong message.

- Women can wear pierced earrings but I would discourage any other piercings.

- Men, I would not suggest wearing any earrings for an interview.

Cologne/Perfume:

- The guideline is that you don't want them to smell you before you enter the room. AND you don't want them to still smell you after you leave.

Nails:

- Make sure your nails look clean and groomed.

- Women, either have no polish or have a professional manicure with light color.

- Women, don't have four-inch-long nails or nails with rhinestones. It will be distracting and send the wrong message.

Briefcases/Purses:

- Bring a regular or portfolio-type briefcase, if possible, with plenty of room for everything. Include paper for notes and a pen that has not been chewed at the top.

- Women, don't bring a purse that is torn or worn out.

When you're done, look in the mirror. Tell yourself you look great! You look professional! You're going to get the job!

"I have to admit, I started out with an attitude about the clothes I should wear. But I learned that this was not the battle to fight. In fact, once I put on a business

suit I felt differently and acted like a professional. I'm

glad I took the extra time."

Student

TO DO

☐ Have three interviewing/networking suits ready, including shoes and jewelry

☐ Purchase an appropriate carrying case for your resume and other items

Chapter 6

Building Relationships

Don't sit home and aggressively wait for the phone to ring

Remember, finding a job is all about "getting out there" and marketing yourself. Take time to review your objectives and target audiences. Finding the right job means meeting and talking to as many people in your "target audience" group as possible. It's not just about the number of people you know but it's also about building quality relationships.

Building relationships means networking. But what does that mean? How do you do it? Sometimes it's a verb, as in "I'm going to network" or "I have to network." Sometimes it's a noun, as in "I'm building my network." I wish someone would have told me early on how important networking is…not only when you're looking for a job but throughout your career.

Networking is about building mutually beneficial relationships, and it is an ongoing tool in your marketing plan. You never know when you'll be back in the market looking for a job or looking to fill a job position in your new company. So keep networking as part of your ongoing career development. The people you meet today, and build relationships with, will be a valuable part of your life tomorrow, professionally and personally.

Step 7: Networking

Now, arm yourself with all the tools that you put together earlier, remember to dress for the job you want, and get out there and network. The best way to get a job is to be prepared and open to new experiences.

Your first networking list is of the people you met in school. Make a list of people in your fraternity or sorority, other classmates, professional organizations, volunteer organizations and classes as well as your professors. Then list all other individuals you may know from team sports, high school and other areas. Write down what these people are doing, where they live and their phone numbers. Let them all know you're looking for work and in what area. And don't forget to ask if there's any way you can help them as well.

Second, take the list of your target markets that you wrote down in Step 3. Then create a list of every association, every event and every charity that would attract this group. Then, practice, practice, practice. As the example displayed in the previous chapter, set up a schedule to attend a certain number of events a week and set up time for follow-up phone calls.

The more you get out and talk to people, hand out your business card, present your elevator pitch and do your follow-up, the better you'll get. Once you start networking over and over again in a specific industry, you will start seeing the same people over and over. This is how you start building relationships.

Networking Events

Remember, while networking can be fun and exhilarating, stay focused on the finish line. It's easy to get caught up in the social rush. You may run into friends and want to drink and catch up, but remember, you're there to meet people who can help with getting a job, so stay professional.

Networking is not only critical for your career now but also for your future. Remember, no company is perfect and you never really know if you have job security so you never know when you'll be back out there or need someone to recommend you.

Preparation Before a Networking Event

- Practice your elevator pitch
- Bring lots of business cards
- Make sure your shoes are polished, nails are polished and speech is polished
- Bring a pen (not one that is chewed at the top) and a small pad of paper
- Bring mints; you don't want to be remembered for

the wrong thing. Chewing gum is a big NO; it never looks good.

- Bring Kleenex

At Networking Events

- Exhibit high energy and a positive attitude
- NEVER speak negatively about another company or other people
- Ask relevant questions when talking to people
- Make sure to listen
- Conduct yourself professionally
- Don't get drunk (people tend to remember poor behavior)
- Don't discuss religion or politics
- Discuss things that will make you stand out (i.e. volunteer work, articles you've written, boards you are on)
- Don't just use people for what you can get; try to help others out as well
- Collect business cards

> **TIP:**
>
> When you attend networking events you will meet a lot of people. The next day, when you're going through the stack of business cards, you may not remember who they were. Immediately after speaking with someone you want to remember, write down information about the person on the back of their business card. You may want to write something like, "first man I met with red tie" or "individual who was in my sorority/fraternity."

After the Networking Event

- Sort through the cards you collected and send a follow-up email within 24 to 48 hours of meeting someone you'd like to talk to further. Set up a time to talk or meet.

- If someone recommended a networking event that you attended, quickly send a thank you note to let the person know it was helpful. This way they will think of you again in the future.

- Remember, people you meet may be generous

and introduce you to new people or companies or opportunities. But at some point you'll have to reciprocate. Otherwise, it can be a small world and you may get a reputation of being a "taker" and that is never good.

Informational Interviews

Occasionally you might meet someone who works for a company you're interested in but you're not really comfortable asking them about job opportunities there. One way to learn more is to ask for an informational interview with someone at their company. People are often open to introducing you to colleagues when there's not the expectation of a job offer at the end. Make sure to do a lot of listening in these informational discussions. They are never a waste. This new connection may even know of someone else at another company who may need help. This is just one more way to market yourself in a different way. And always make sure to send a thank you note to the person interviewing you as well as the person who set you up.

Networking Opportunities

Here is a list of networking opportunities that you can look into right now. There are hundreds of others, but this is a start:

- Volunteering

- Chambers of commerce

- Toastmasters meetings

- Job fairs

- Business conferences

- Alumni events or career days at your university

- Professional associations affiliated with your area of expertise

- Conventions

TIP:

At conventions you have the ability to go booth to booth and connect with multiple companies. Make sure one of the days you attend a convention is the first day it opens. People tend to be energized and eager to talk. Plus, most managers attend the first day, so you may be able to connect with the head of the specific department that you want to work in.

"When I first started attending networking events, it felt awkward. I would stand along the side of the room and watch. Then I started to go up to people and introduce myself. As it turned out, most people felt uncomfortable and appreciated me approaching them."

Student

TIP:

Getting involved with a charity is a wonderful way to meet people. You're in an environment that is good for your image, and it's less formal than an actual networking program. It's a great way to make new friends AND business connections. It also gives you an opportunity to practice your pitch. And it feels good to do something for others.

TO DO

☐ Make a list of all current contacts

☐ Make a list of networking opportunities

☐ Research your school for job opportunities

Chapter 7

Interviewing

It's very exciting, and scary, to go on job interviews. Remember, it is about marketing YOU as the product.

Step 8: The Interview

Below are some quick tips on marketing yourself in the interview process:

Practice, Practice, Practice

Just like sports, being ready for interviews takes practice, practice, practice. You don't go on the football field and play against another team on the first day. You spend weeks/months/years training, limbering up and doing practice games with your own team. It's like that in the job interviewing world as well.

> **TIP:**
> I've heard people say that if you are nervous going on your first interviews, practice with companies that are not your first choice. Of course something great can come of these too, but the point is to use these as your practice set. It gives you a chance to see how you feel, get used to the process, understand the questions asked and test your pitch. This way you've limbered up just like in sports and you are ready to talk to companies that you are interested in working for.

A day or two before the interview...

PREPARATION

- Learn about the company ahead of time so you can speak intelligently to the interviewer; it will impress them. This includes learning about and understanding the company's competition.

- Be aware of what benefits they are offering and what you'd like to have in your package. Salary is just one aspect of what you should be looking for from a company. Gain a solid understanding about taxes, profit sharing, 401(k) savings, pension and health insurance before going into any interview. These may not be important for the first interview, but eventually you will need to discuss this intelligently.

- Have your business cards in a card case, your resume in a folder, two pens (in case one doesn't work) and paper for notes.

- Rehearse the answers to basic questions that may be asked of you (remember to look at Step 1 and Step 2 to formulate your answers)

EXAMPLE

INTERVIEW QUESTIONS

What are your professional strengths?
What skills do you have?
What are you looking for in a job?
Where do you see yourself in five years?
Why should we hire you?

- Be ready to discuss other things you do such as volunteer work, summer jobs and blogs or articles you've written on topics related to your area of interest.

- Make sure your clothes are ironed.

- Get enough sleep.

Arriving at the Interview

- Approach every interview as if it were the most important one. Maintain high energy and enthusiasm.

- Never be late. In fact, arrive at least 10 minutes early. It is better to wait for the interviewer then to make them wait for you.

- If you HAVE to be late, call and let them know when you'll be there, even if it's just five minutes later than scheduled. It will show you care. BUT, just don't be late.

- Throw out your gum before you enter the building.

- Be nice and respectful to everyone. Be nice to the security guard. Be especially nice to the receptionist and office support individuals. The receptionist can be your best source of information down the road.

- Turn off your cell phone and/or your Blackberry before arriving.

- Do not text message during the interview, even in the waiting room or afterward walking out of the meeting. Wait until you leave the building.

- Maintain good posture in the waiting room. Remember, how you look when they come to greet you creates their first impression.

- When you are greeted for the interview, stand up, shake the person's hand (firmly) and look them in the eye.

During the Interview

- Display good posture.

- Use proper English (don't use "yep," "nope" or "like")

- Show high energy.

- Go in with 100% confidence that you're excited, willing and loyal.

- For the first interview, don't ask about what time the job starts each day or what time the day ends. And don't ask if they are flexible about the hours.

- Be a good listener. You may think you're a good listener but when you're nervous and someone asks you to talk about yourself, it's easy to get excited and keep talking. You don't want to miss hearing what they are looking for in a candidate.

- If someone enters the room during the interview and you are introduced to this person, stand up and shake their hand.

- Never talk negatively about any other company you have worked for, even if it was part-time or a summer job. It says something to this employer about your loyalty.

- Never talk negatively about other co-workers you've

worked with either.

- Don't discuss how you were out late the night before or if you got drunk with friends.

- Don't ask about jobs for friends on an interview.

- Don't say you are only looking for a stepping stone until you decide what you want to do.

- Don't tell a company what's wrong with it.

- Don't flirt with people in the office.

- Don't fidget or click a pen.

- Do ask the person speaking to you for a business card.

- Don't discuss religion or politics.

- Ask interviewers how they'd like you to communicate with them (i.e. by email or phone).

"I've interviewed hundreds of individuals over the years and the ones with good manners always stand out."

Hiring Manager

After the Interview

- Once you leave the building, write down the questions they asked you before you forget. This way you can use them as a guideline for your next interview.

- Immediately send a thank you note to everyone you interviewed with. If you want to send an email first, that's fine but a note should follow. And don't use text messages or text message abbreviations when writing.

- If you haven't heard back within a week or two, you can make a follow-up phone call. Remember, people do get busy so don't despair. And remember to sound pleasant on the phone.

- Don't forget the people who have been helpful. Always send a thank you note if someone connected you with that contact, even if it doesn't result in a job.

If You Don't Get the Job

If the interview doesn't go well or you don't get the job, that's okay. Learn from each one and move forward. Don't dwell on the bad things. Also, even if you don't get a particular job at a company, others may open up down the road that you receive a call about in the future. Something better is always waiting ahead.

> *"I interviewed with a company I really wanted to work for. Unfortunately, I didn't get that particular job but I still liked the company. So every month I sent an email to my contact just checking in and letting them know I was still interested. At four months they contacted me and I ended up getting a job in a different department."*
>
> *Job Search Applicant*

TO DO

☐ Practice your answers to interview questions

☐ Get enough sleep the night before an interview

☐ Remember to follow up and thank interviewers

Chapter 8

Nix the Naysayers

Looking for a job is not only physical, it's mental. A good mental attitude is critical. What does that mean? There are individuals who will tell you "It's impossible to get a job" and that "No one is hiring." Even if the economy were strong right now, there would be those naysayers who would say "You can't get that job because you didn't go to the right university" or "You didn't get the best grades" or "You don't know the right people." The point is, there are always reasons why things aren't "perfect." Ignore these negative thoughts and keep moving. It takes tenacity, focus and strategy to get where you want to go. And if you see a pothole in the road, go around it or figure out a way to fix it. Don't let it stop the journey.

You will do great. You can get a job. You will get a job. Just stay on course with your marketing plan.

Step 9: Clean House

Clean house of naysayers and other toxic individuals.

In other words, don't let others determine your future. While friends and family may have your best interests at heart, they may not be giving you the best information. Some may tell you that you don't need to wear a suit for an interview. Don't listen. Some may text message you during an interview. Don't respond. Some may tell you to take any job just so you're employed. Some may say that you'll never get a job in your field and the market is terrible. Remember, you've read this book and know what you need to do. It's important to stay positive and keep telling yourself that things will be fine and continue to persevere. The strong, determined and best will win.

Your self worth does not depend on how many interviews you've had or how many call backs you get.

There will always be friends who turn the job search into

a competitive sport. They tell you how many interviews they've been on and how many call backs they've gotten and ask you the same. Don't fall into this pattern. There will always be that one friend or acquaintance who will get the first job, big paycheck, great vacation package and bonus...great, great, great. Remember, you're not in a classroom boxed in with 50 other students. You are your own brand, and that means you're different from others. This is your personal product you're selling, so stay steady and don't compare scorecards. Be happy for their success, but don't let these people drag you down.

Beware of people stealing information.

Be careful how much information you share with friends. You're all out there looking for a job. And an innocent comment to a friend that they share with someone else can cost you your competitive edge. Also, your friend, as close as you are, may find a job you interviewed with as interesting as you did and go behind your back...or mention it to someone else who has no loyalties to you.

"I made the mistake of telling a friend at lunch about my great job interview I had that morning. I didn't stop there. I told her the company name and the person I interviewed with and the title of the position. She innocently mentioned it to a friend of hers and they slid in and stole it from me. I learned a valuable lesson."

Student

Don't let your ego get in the way.

Great grades, a great college and great recommendations won't necessarily guarantee you a job. Marketing yourself as professional, well rounded, interesting and eager will.

Don't speak negatively about ANYONE.

Once you're out looking for work, the world gets very small. People in the same industry tend to know each other, and everyone talks. So if you come back from a bad interview and start talking negatively about a person at a particular company, there's a chance someone could know them and word could get back.

TIP:

Once you've experienced some rejections, or if weeks go by with no feedback, you may start feeling bad. It's human nature. And you may start telling people around you. This is also human nature. While it's okay to talk to a few close confidants, try not to do this too much. While people may want to help, dwelling on the negative only makes it worse.

"Everyone made fun of me when I spent my days in December trying to get a job. People told me I'd never get a job in the month of December. They said it's the holidays and no one hires at the holidays and I shouldn't waste my time. I wanted to work, I needed to work. So I spent double the time and ended up getting a job the day before Christmas and started January 2nd."

Manager

TO DO

☐ Think about the individuals in your life who are a negative force

☐ Think about the individuals in your life who are a positive force

Chapter 9

Remember the Things You Were Taught When You Were Little

Step 10: Simple Rules

Below are some simple rules that you should follow. None of these will be foreign to you, and most you've heard before. This is just a reminder. AND they are in no particular order.

- Be nice, polite and respectful to EVERYONE...*even if you don't like them*

- Shake everyone's hand when you meet them...*make it a firm handshake*...and look them in the eye

- Call people Mr. or Ms. unless told otherwise

- Always look your best

- Think about what you say before you say it...*and how you say it*

- Don't speak negatively about people

- Not everyone likes to be contacted via email or text

or even by phone ...*ask for their preference*

- Say "please," "thank you," and "you're welcome"

- Be organized

- Return all calls

- Make sure all email correspondence is complete (no sentence fragments, or incomplete sentences), grammatically correct and spell checked

- Be patient

- Always be on time

- Turn off your cell phone and/or your Blackberry when meeting/talking with someone

- Thank people who have been helpful in your job search...and your life

- Be loyal

- Persevere

- Stay focused, driven and energized

- Drink lots of water, eat right, get enough sleep and

exercise…these things will put you at the top of your game!

"When I first went out to look for a job, I felt like I had no control over anything I was doing. Once I put my job search plan in place, I felt empowered and in control. I moved forward with confidence and energy."

Student

~~THE END~~

THE BEGINNING

Conclusion

Final Thoughts

There is so much to learn and remember when you are involved in the job search process. This book is set up as a reference guide. Keep it available at all times during your job search effort and remember to:

- Refer to this book when you're putting together your toolkit

- Refer to this book every time you go to a networking event as a reminder of what to bring, say and do

- Refer to this book when you're going on an interview to give you that competitive edge each time

- Re-read the TIPS, examples and quotes from time to time to remind you that it is about marketing yourself when you're looking for a job

As mentioned earlier in the book, marketing YOU as the product is about being the one that people remember when there's a job opportunity because you stood out for the right reasons. Thinking and acting strategically in this process will keep you ahead of the competition. Marketing yourself is about image, perception and reputation.

Build your job search marketing plan and leave nothing to chance. These ten steps that you just read about will help in making your plan strategic. They are:

- Step 1: Decide on your image and make sure the image you want and the image you have are in sync.

- Step 2: Make a list of your skills and your strengths to gain an edge over the competition.

- Step 3: Make sure you have a finish line, or a destination, and a plan on how to get there. Target the audience, the individuals or companies, at your finish line in everything you do.

- Step 4: As an ongoing part of your plan, insert a measurement system. If the results don't align with the finish line, change course.

- Step 5: Gather the tools you will need and build your toolkit. This includes business cards, voicemail, phone message, email address, resume, cover letter, thank you notes, elevator pitch, job search log, time management chart and your online presence.

- Step 6: First impressions are important and your appearance should create the right image. This includes clothing, hair, jewelry, shoes, briefcase/ purse, nails and your cologne/perfume.

- Step 7: Don't sit home and aggressively wait for the phone to ring. Finding a job is all about marketing yourself and building relationships. And building relationships means networking. Remember to be prepared before, during and after the networking event.

- Step 8: The job interview is just as strategic as the rest of your plan. Therefore, you need to practice and prepare prior to the interview, stay focused and on point during the interview and follow up after the interview.

- Step 9: It takes tenacity, focus and strategy to get

where you want to go so clean house of naysayers and other toxic individuals. Don't let negative individuals stop your journey. A good mental attitude is critical.

- Step 10: Remember the simple rules that will get you through life. Here's a sample of the critical ones:

  – Be nice, polite and respectful to EVERYONE

  – Stay focused, driven and energized

  – Always look your best

  – Be loyal

  – Don't speak negatively about people

Marketing Yourself to the Real World...

...a new start, a new world, a new experience.

For more information or to contact Susan Caplan about speaking at your next event, visit the website:

www.susancaplan.com